AUTOMATIC MAIN POWER AND APPLIANCES CONTROL

AMPAC

VIMALRAJ S

Contents

ABSTRACT

The recent technology in home automation provides security, safety and comfortable life at home. That is why in the competitive environment and fast world, home automation technology is required for every person. This is made up of both automatic and manual mode.

This purposed home automation technology provides smart monitoring and control of the home appliances. The control and monitoring the status have been implemented using The Internet Of Things (IOT), Contactors, Relays, MCB, DPDT switch, Push buttons and Multi Function Meter(MFM).

The system has low-cost design, user friendly interface, and easy installation in home or multi-purpose building. Using this technology, the consumer can reduce the wastage of electrical power by regular monitoring of home appliances or the proper ON/OFF scheduling of the devices.

LIST OF ABBREVIATIONS

PIC

Peripheral Interface Controller

GSM

Global System for Mobile communication

LCD

Liquid Crystal Display

LDR

Light Dependent Resistor

FPPS

Fingerprint Pressure Sensor

LCD

Liquid Crystal Display

CHAPTER ONE

INTRODUCTION

Electricity is the most basic need of everyone in this modern world. Energy consumption graph is increasing day by day whereas the resources of energy are diminishing parallel. Usage of power is growing drastically paving the way for energy efficient technologies and digging for renewable energy sources.

Since prevention is better than cure awareness of energy consumption should be brought into every place before resources get extinguished. Industrial users consume about 37 percent of the total energy, personal and commercial transportation consumes 20 percent whereas residential appliances consume 11 percent; and commercial uses amount to 5 percent of the total energy and remaining 27 percent of the world's energy is lost in energy transmission and generation.

The process of controlling or operating various equipment, machinery, industrial processes, and other applications using various control systems and also with less or no human intervention is termed as automation. There are various types of automation based on the application they can be categorized as home automation, industrial automation, autonomous automation, building automation. In this the automation is done using Internet of Things (IOT).

Automatic Main Power Appliances and Control using IOT is an innovative application of internet of things developed to control home appliances remotely over the cloud. The home automation system project can be developed by following simple steps shown below. The essential components and materials for home automation using IOT project can be listed as a Wi-Fi module, RF module, Transformer, resistors, capacitors, diode, regulator, loads.

CHAPTER TWO

LITERATURE SURVEY

The AMPAC system that uses Wi-Fi technology. System consists of three main components; web server, which presents system core that controls, and monitors users' home and hardware interface module which provides appropriate interface to sensors and actuator of AMPAC system. The System is better from the scalability and flexibility point of view than the commercially available home automation systems. If system is connected to the internet, so remote users can access server web based application through the internet.

Application developed using the Android platform controlled and monitored from a remote location using the smart home app. The sensors and actuators/relays are directly interfaced to the main controller. Proposed design offers are the control of energy management systems such as lightings, heating, air conditioning, security, fire detection and intrusion detection with an alarm sound.

Internet of Things is the controller used to control the appliances by using GSM technology. It uses certain peripheral drivers and relays to achieve this interfacing. The application on smart phone generates SMS messages based on the user commands and sends it to the mobile phone and control the home appliances. The system has drawbacks of cost and reliability of SMS. An interface cannot be customized based on devices.

AMPAC satisfies the resident's needs and desires by adjustable light, temperature, ambient music, automatic shading, safety & security, even arrangement of wire. Home automation technologies are the latest fascination with housing mechanism. However, with the appearance of new electronic technologies and their combination with older, traditional building technologies, the smart home is at last becoming a reality.

CHAPTER THREE

BLOCK DIAGRAM

3.1 BLOCK DIAGRAM FOR POWER CIRCUIT

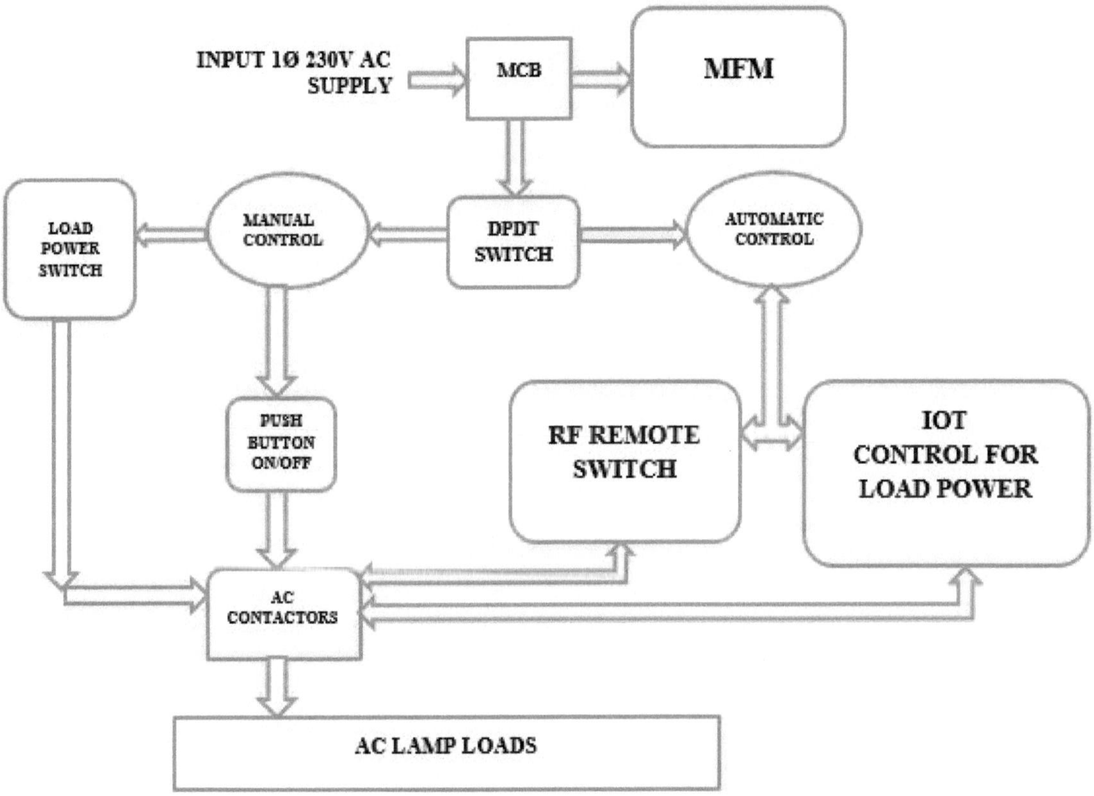

3.2 BLOCK DIAGRAM FOR CONTROL CIRCUIT

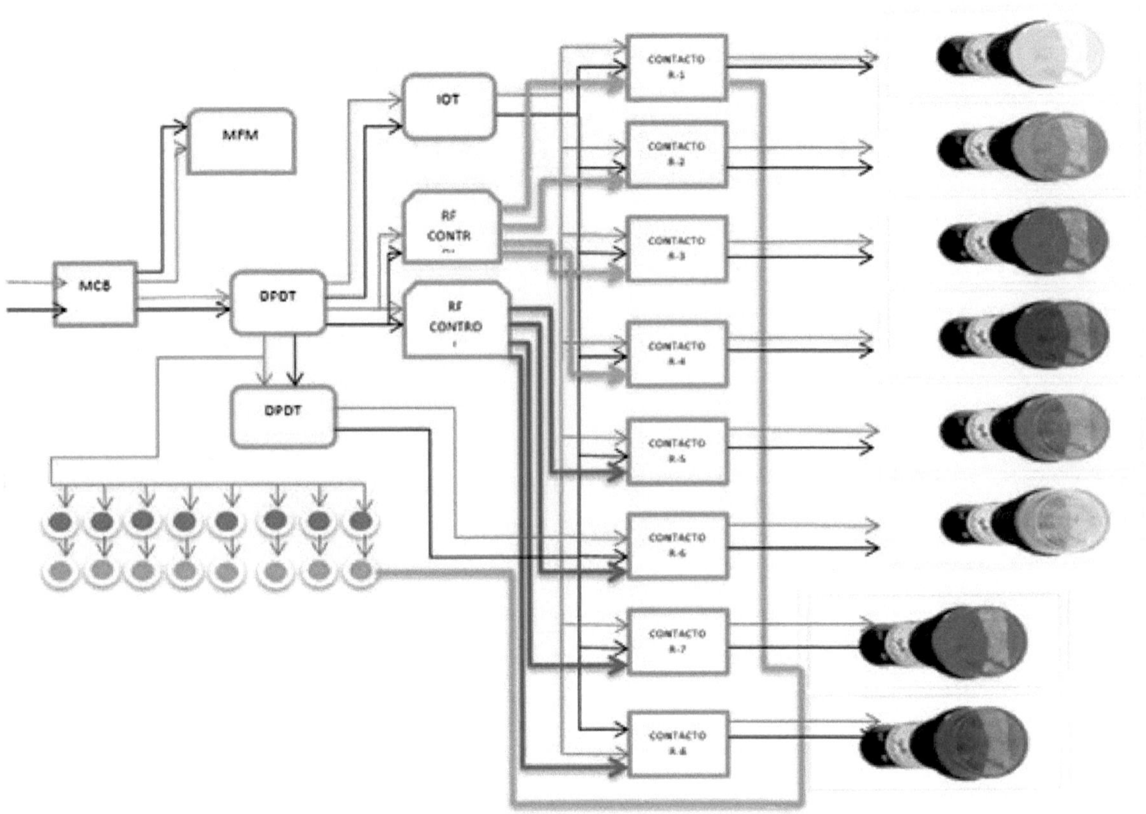
MFM
IOT
MCB
DPDT
RF
CONTR
RF
CONTRO
DPDT

CHAPTER FOUR

MCB

4.1. CORE FEATURES

MCBs or Miniature Circuit Breakers are electromechanical devices which protect an electrical circuit from an over current. The over current, in an electrical circuit, may result from short circuit, overload or faulty design. In order to restart the flow of current the MCB is manually turned on. A wide variety of MCBs have been in use nowadays with breaking capacity of 10KA to 16 KA, in all areas of domestic, commercial and industrial applications as a reliable means of protection.

MCBs are of time delay tripping devices, to which the magnitude of overcurrent controls the operating time. This means, these get operated whenever overload exist long enough to create a danger to the circuit being protected. Therefore, MCBs doesn't respond to transient loads such as switches surges and motor starting currents.

MCBs are manufactured in different pole versions such as single, double, triple and four pole structures with different fault current levels. MCB operates as a switch (manual one) to make the circuit ON or OFF. Under overload or short circuit condition, it automatically operates or trips so that current interruption takes place in the load circuit. The visual indication of this trip can be observed by automatic movement of the operating knob to OFF position.

In overload condition, the current through the bimetal causes to raise the temperature of it. The heat generated within the bimetal itself enough to cause deflection due to thermal expansion of metals. This deflection further releases the trip latch and hence contacts get separated.

In this project type D MCB is used. It will trip instantly at a rate of ten to twenty five times its rated current. These are normally used for very high inductive loads where high inrush current are very frequent. These are suitable for specific industrial and commercial applications. The common examples of such applications include x-ray machines, UPS systems, industrial welding equipment, large winding motors, etc.

This type of MCB causes frequent tripping and causes to interrupt the current to the load it is being connected, because the MCB nominal current less than nominal current value of the load. Similarly, if it is oversized the load to it is connected will not be protected efficiently. In such case, the MCB will not trip even though load is drawing over currents.

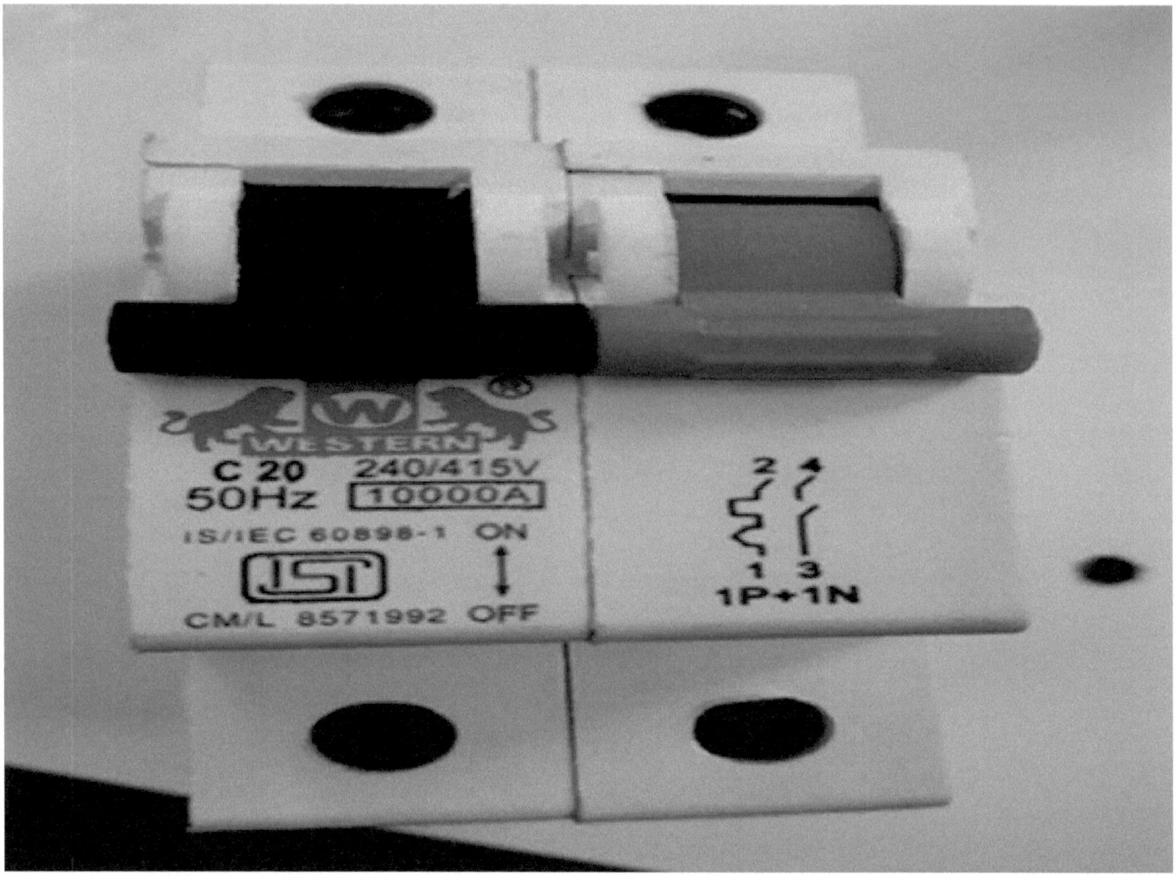

FIG 4.1 SINGLE PHASE MCB

CHAPTER FIVE

MULTI FUNCTION METER

5.1. CORE FEATURES

The Multi Function Meter is made to fulfil this requirement. The Multi Function Meter consist of 16 characters 4 line LCD display for displaying parameters. The Multi Function Meter is capable of displaying total parameters. The Multi Function Meter has facility to select CT Secondary on site. The integration time for maximum demand calculation is also site selectable.

To display the various parameters Multi-Function meter uses a backlight illuminated 20 x 4 characters Liquid Crystal Display. This helps to display three phase parameters in one screen.

Operation of Multi Function Meter is very simple and easy to understand. It operates in two modes Auto Mode and Manual Mode. These digital panel meters measure all electrical qualities like Voltage, current, Power, energy, Frequency & Power Factor accurately.

FIG 5.1 MULTIFUNCTION METER

CHAPTER SIX

DPDT SWITCH

6.1 CORE FEATURES:

DPDT switch means Adding another pole to the SPDT creates a double-pole, double-throw switch. Basically two SPDT switches, which can control two separate circuits, but are always switched together by a single actuator. DPDTs should have six terminals.

A Single Pole Single Throw toggle switch connects or disconnects one terminal either to or from another. It is the simplest switch. A DPDT switch works just like two separate SPDT switches attached to the same switch bat. A Double Pole Double Throw switch is a switch that has 2 inputs and 4 outputs; each input has 2 corresponding outputs that it can connect to.

Each of the terminals of a double pole double switch can either be in 1 of 2 positions. This makes the the double pole double throw switch a very versatile switch. With 2 inputs, it can connect to 4 different outputs. It can reroute a circuit into 2 different modes of operation.

A Double Pole Double Throw Switch is actually two single pole double throw switches.

A DPDT switch allows a circuit to be in 1 of 2 modes. When the DPDT switch is switched one way the lamp and buzzer are both on, while the LED and speaker are off. When the DPDT switch is switched the other way the LED and the speaker are both on, while the lamp and buzzer are off.

DPDT switches have the dynamic 2-mode capacity that allows control of 4 different devices.

FIG 6.1 DPDT SWITCH

CHAPTER SEVEN

INTERNET OF THINGS

7.1. CORE FEATURES

Internet of Things provides remote connectivity using internet facility. It is a one channel operation it provides security. It can be accessed anywhere through mobile. An IOT system consists of sensors/devices which is connected to the cloud through some kind of connectivity. Once the data gets to the cloud, software processes it and then might decide to perform an action, such as sending an alert or automatically adjusting the sensors/devices without the need for the user.

The Internet of Things is a system of physical things embedded with sensors, software, electronics and connectivity to allow it to perform better by exchanging information with other connected devices, the operator or the manufacturer.

The IOT allows objects to be sensed or controlled remotely across existing network infrastructure, creating opportunities for more direct integration of the physical world into computer-based systems, and resulting in improved efficiency, accuracy and economic benefit in addition to reduced human intervention.

A growing portion of IOT devices are created for consumer use. Consumer applications include connected car, entertainment, home automation wearable technology, quantified self, connected health, and appliances such as washer, dryers, robotic vacuums, air purifiers, ovens, or refrigerators/freezers that use Wi-Fi for remote monitoring. Consumer IOT provides new opportunities for user experience and interfaces.

These home systems utilize assistive technology to accommodate an owner's specific disabilities. Voice control can assist users with sight and mobility limitations while alert systems can be connected directly to Cochlear implants worn by hearing impaired users.They can also be equipped with additional safety features. These features can include sensors that monitor for medical emergencies such as falls or seizures. Smart home technology applied in this way can provide users with more freedom and a higher quality of life.

7.2. Applications

- Lighting control
- HVAC
- Lawn/Gardening management
- Smart Home Appliances
- Improved Home safety and security
- Home air quality and water quality monitoring
- Natural Language-based voice assistants
- Better Infotainment delivery
- AI-driven digital experiences
- Smart Switches
- Smart Locks
- Smart Energy Meters

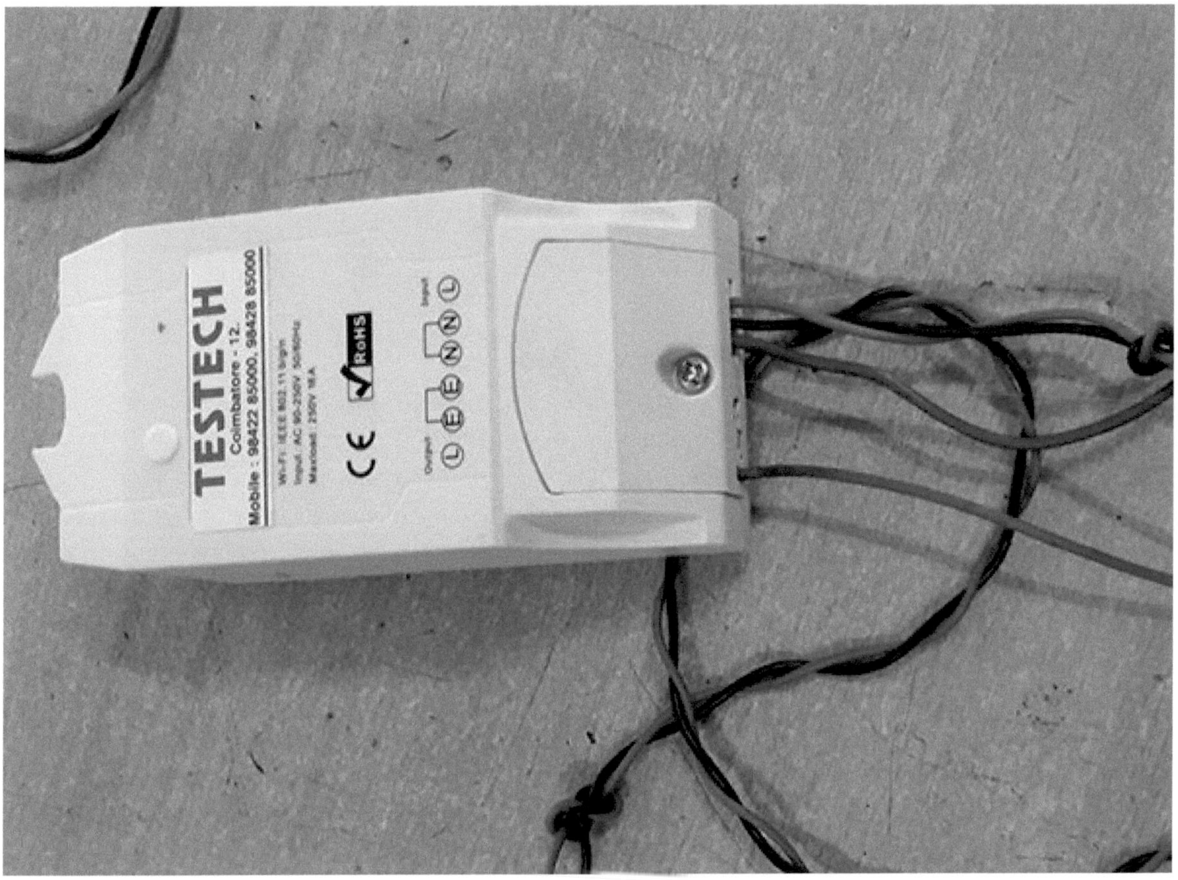

7.1 IOT DEVICE

CHAPTER EIGHT

AUTO

8.1. CORE FEATURES

An RF module is a small electronic device used to transmit and/or receive radio signals between two devices. In an embedded system it is often desirable to communicate with another device wirelessly.

RF modules are most often used in medium and low volume products for consumer applications such as garage door openers, wireless alarm or monitoring systems, industrial remote controls, smart sensor applications, and wireless home automation systems. They are sometimes used to replace older infra red communication designs as they have the advantage of not requiring line-of-sight operation.

The carrier frequencies are commonly used in commercially available RF modules, including those in the industrial, scientific and medical radio bands such as 433.92 MHz, 915 MHz, and 2400 MHz These frequencies are used because of national and international regulations governing the used of radio for communication. Short Range Devices may also use frequencies available for unlicensed such as 315 MHz and 868 MHz.

The term RF module can be applied to many different types, shapes and sizes of small electronic sub assembly circuit board. It can also be applied to modules across a huge variation of functionality and capability. RF modules typically incorporate a printed circuit board, transmit or receive circuit, antenna, and serial interface for communication to the host processor.

8.2. RF MODULE

A transmitter is an electronic device which produces radio waves with the help of an antenna. A transmitter generates a radio frequency current applied to the antenna, which in turn radiates radio waves. A transmitter generates radio waves for communication.

An RF transmitter module is a small PCB sub-assembly capable of transmitting a radio wave and modulating that wave to carry data. Transmitter modules are usually implemented alongside a micro controller which will provide data to the module which can be transmitted. RF transmitters are usually subject to regulatory requirements which dictate the maximum allowable transmitter power output, harmonics, and band edge requirements.

A transmitter can either be a separate piece of electronic equipment or an integrated circuit within another electronic device. Most transmitters are used for radio communication of information over a certain distance. The information that is provided to the transmitter is in the form of an electronic signal. This includes audio from a microphone, video from a TV camera, or a digital signal for wireless networking devices. The transmitter combines the information signal that is to be carried with the RF signal which generates the radio waves. This is called modulation.

In an FM transmitter, the information is added to the radio signal by slightly varying the radio signal's frequency. In an AM transmitter, it is added by varying its amplitude. Several other types of modulation are also used. ICs, or integrated circuits, allow high performance circuits to be built at lesser costs and with significant amounts of space savings.

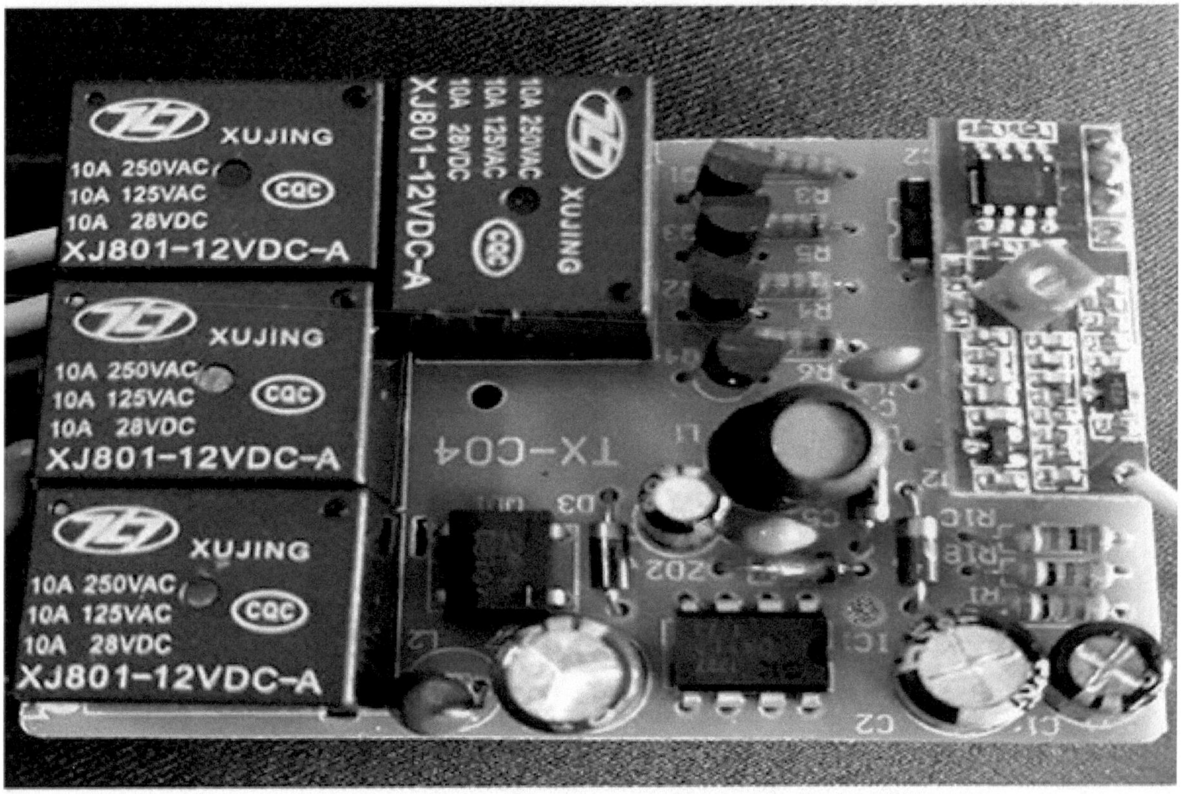

FIG 8.1 RF RECIEVER MODULE

8.3. PIN DIAGRAM OF HT12D

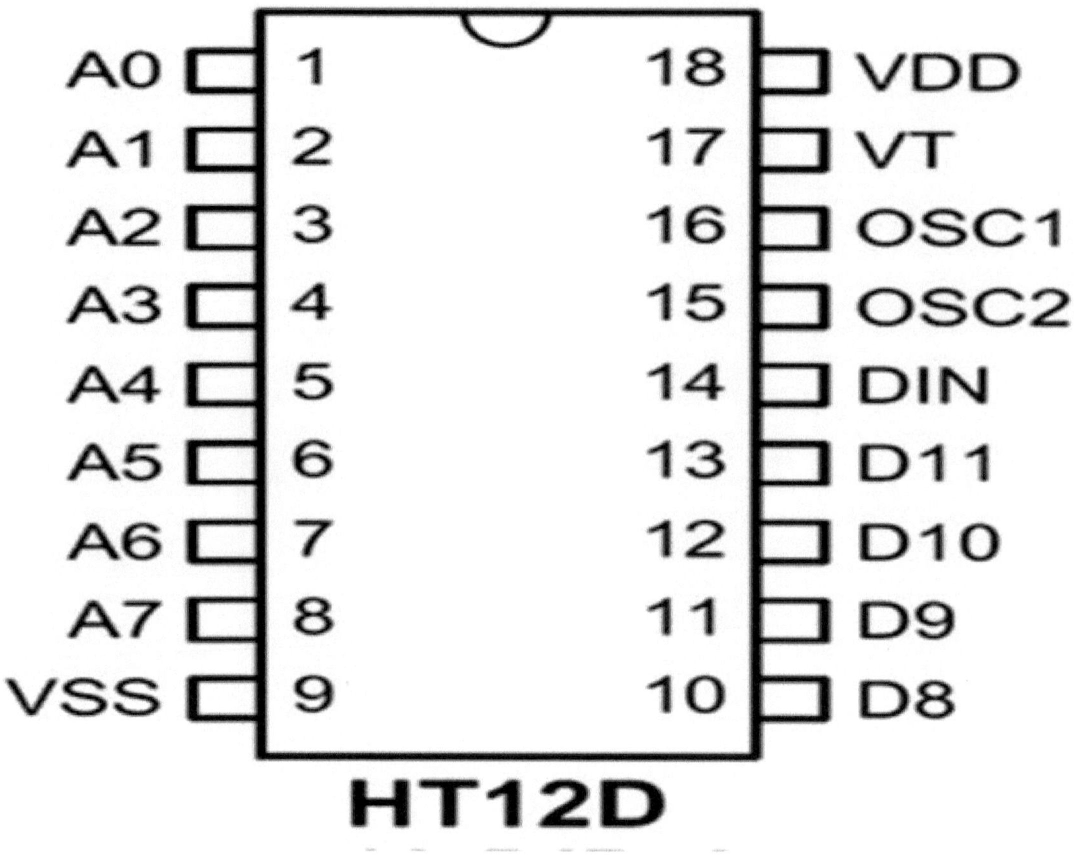

8.4. PIN DESCRIPTION

Pin No	Function	Name
1	8 bit Address pins for input	A0
2		A1
3		A2
4		A3
5		A4
6		A5
7		A6
8		A7
9	Ground (0V)	Ground
10	4 bit Data/Address pins for output	D0
11		D1
12		D2
13		D3
14	Serial data input	Input
15	Oscillator output	Osc2
16	Oscillator input	Osc1
17	Valid transmission; active high	VT
18	Supply voltage; 5V (2.4V-12V)	Vcc

8.5 FEATURES

- Operating voltage: 2.4V~12V
- Low power and high noise immunity CMOS technology
- Low stand-by current
- Capable of decoding 12 bits of information
- Pairs with HOLTEK's 212 series of encoders
- Binary address setting
- Three times of receiving check Address/Data number combination HT12D:8 address bits and 4 data bits – HT12F: 12 address bits and 0 data bit
- A built-in oscillator with only a 5% resistor
- A valid transmission indicator
- Easy interface with an RF or an Infra-Red transmission medium
- Minimal external components

8.6. PIN DIAGRAM OF HT12E

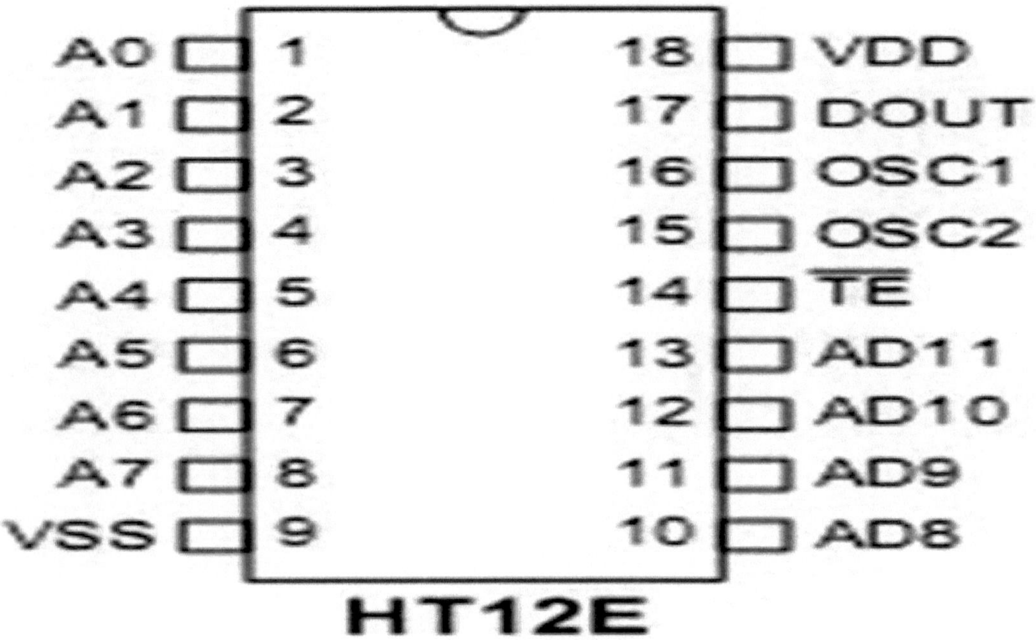

8.7.PIN DESCRIPTION

Pin No	Function	Name
1	8 bit Address pins for input	A0
2		A1
3		A2
4		A3
5		A4
6		A5
7		A6
8		A7
9	Ground (0V)	Ground
10	4 bit Data/Address pins for input	AD0
11		AD1
12		AD2
13		AD3
14	Transmission enable; active low	TE
15	Oscillator input	Osc2
16	Oscillator output	Osc1
17	Serial data output	Output
18	Supply voltage; 5V (2.4V-12V)	Vcc

Enter Caption

8.8 FEATURES

- Operating voltage: 2.4V~12V
- Low power and high noise immunity CMOS technology
- Low stand-by current
- Capable of decoding 12 bits of information
- Pairs with HOLTEK's 212 series of encoders
- Binary address setting
- Three times of receiving check Address/Data number combination HT12D:8 address bits and 4 data bits – HT12F: 12 address bits and 0 data bit
- A built-in oscillator with only a 5% resistor
- A valid transmission indicator
- Easy interface with an RF or an Infra-Red transmission medium
- Minimal external components

8.9 CIRCUIT DIAGRAM

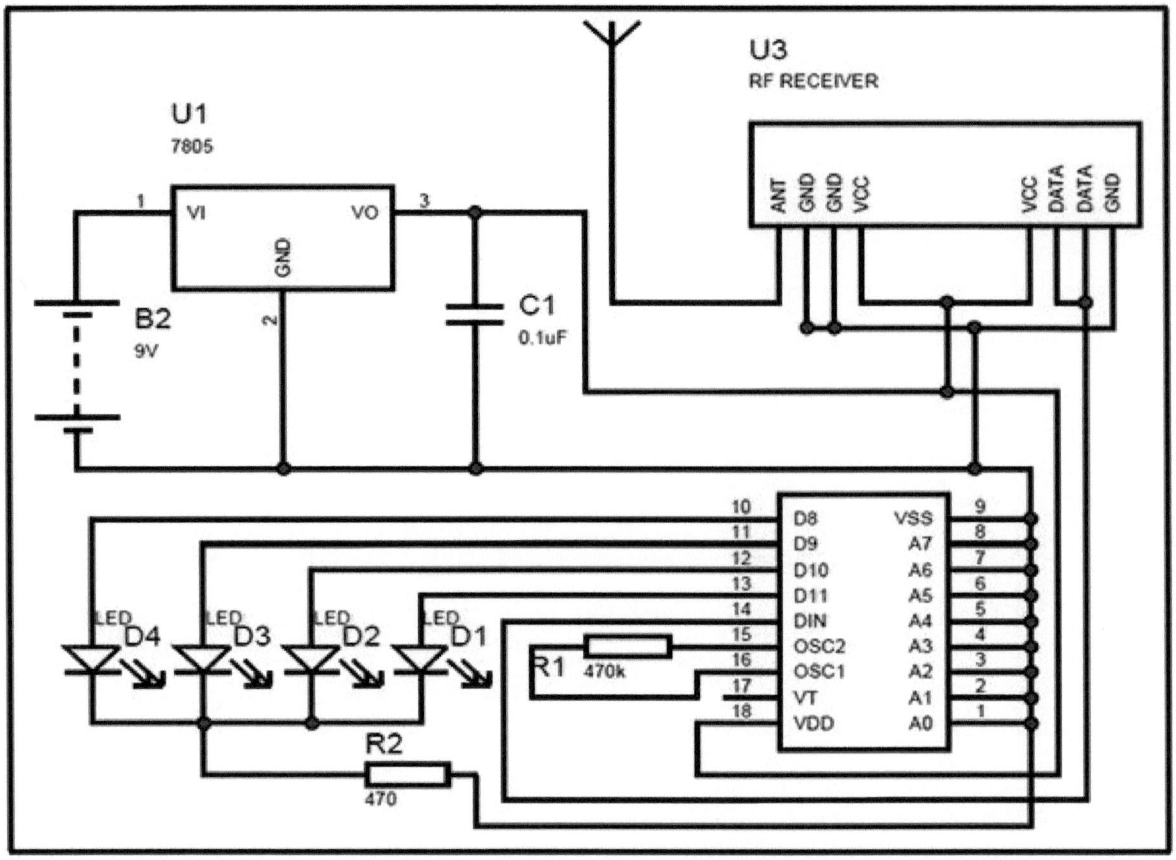
U3
RF RECEIVER
ANT
GND
GND
VCC
VCC
DATA
DATA
GND
U1
7805
VI
VO
GND
B2
9V
C1
0.1uF
D8
D9
D10
D11
DIN
OSC2
OSC1
VT
VDD
VSS
A7
A6
A5
A4
A3
A2
A1
A0
LED
D4
D3
D2
D1
R1
470k
R2
470

CHAPTER NINE

RELAY

9.1 CORE FEATURES

A relay is an electrical device. Many relays is use an electromagnet to mechanically operate a switch, but other operating principles are also used, such as solid-state relays. Relays are used where it is necessary to control a circuit by a separate low-power signal, or where several circuits must be controlled by one signal. The first relays were used in long distance telegraph circuits as amplifiers: they repeated the signal coming in from one circuit and re-transmitted it on another circuit. Relays were used extensively in telephone exchanges and early computers to perform logical operations. In this system both Transmitter and Receiver is used.

An RF transmitter module is a small PCB sub-assembly capable of transmitting a radio wave and modulating that wave to carry data. Transmitter modules are usually implemented alongside a micro controller which will provide data to the module which can be transmitted. RF transmitters are usually subject to regulatory requirements which dictate the maximum allowable transmitter power output, harmonics, and band edge requirements.

An RF receiver module receives the modulated RF signal, and demodulates it. There are two types of RF receiver modules super heterodyne receivers and super-regenerative receivers. Super heterodyne receivers have a performance advantage over super-regenerative; they offer increased accuracy and stability over a large voltage and temperature range. This stability comes from a fixed crystal design which in the past tended to mean a comparatively more expensive product.

Relays provide an easy way to control large AC and DC loads and device. With the 315MHz RF receiver integrated in, it can be directly remote controlled by the matching transmitter controller, which make it easy to use in home automation and industry control. The relay receiver board must be provided with 12 DC supply to get it work the transmitter controller has its own battery.

JQC-3FF-S-Z
10A 250VAC
15A 125VAC
10A 250VAC
5VDC
TONGLING
VCC GND IN

9:1 RELAY

CHAPTER TEN

PUSH BUTTON

10.1. CORE FEATURES

A push-button is a simple switch mechanism for controlling some aspect of a machine or a process. Buttons are typically made out of hard material, usually plastic or metal. The surface is usually flat or shaped to accommodate the human finger or hand, so as to be easily depressed or pushed.

In industrial and commercial applications, push buttons can be connected together by a mechanical linkage so that the act of pushing one button causes the other button to be released. In this way, a stop button can "force" a start button to be released. This method of linkage is used in simple manual operations in which the machine or process has no electrical circuits for control.

NO is normally open i.e. the contacts are normally open and close when the switch is actuated. NC is normally closed i.e. the contacts are normally closed and open when the switch is actuated. 1NO1NC is generally used to describe contactors and manual switches like emergency stop button.

An "open" circuit is an incomplete circuit, with "open space" between contacts. Therefore a normally open circuit can also be referred to as "normally OFF". A normally closed or N.C. momentary switch has one or more circuits that are closed when the switch actuator is at its normal or rest position.

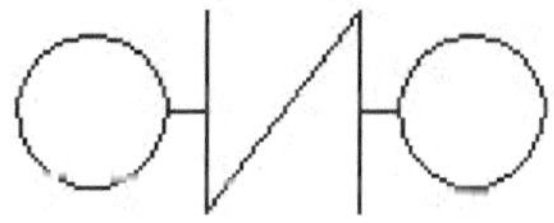

NO

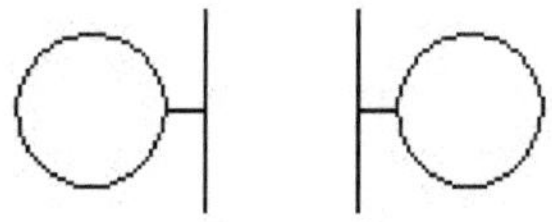

NC

10.2. APPLICATIONS

- Calculators
- Push-button
- Telephones
- Kitchen appliances
- Magnetic locks

- Mechanical and Electronic devices,
- Home and Commercial.

10.1 PUSH BUTTON

CHAPTER ELEVEN

CONTACTOR

11.1. CORE FEATURES

When current passes through the electromagnet, a magnetic field is produced this attracts the moving core of the contactor. The electromagnet coil draws more current initially, until its inductance increases when the metal core enters the coil. The moving contact is propelled by the moving core; the force developed by the electromagnet holds the moving and fixed contacts together. When the contactor coil is de-energized, gravity or a spring returns the electromagnet core to its initial position and opens the contacts.

For contactors energized with alternating current, a small part of the core is surrounded with a shading coil, which slightly delays the magnetic flux in the core. The effect is to average out the alternating pull of the magnetic field and so prevent the core from buzzing at twice line frequency.

Because arcing and consequent damage occurs just as the contacts are opening or closing, contactors are designed to open and close very rapidly there is often an internal tipping point mechanism to ensure rapid action.

Rapid closing can, however, lead to increase contact bounce which causes additional unwanted open-close cycles. One solution is to have bifurcated contacts to minimize contact bounce; two contacts designed to close simultaneously, but bounce at different times so the circuit will not be briefly disconnected and cause an arc.

A slight variant has multiple contacts designed to engage in rapid succession. The first to make contact and last to break will experience the greatest contact wear and will form a high-resistance connection that would cause excessive heating inside the contactor. However, in doing so, it will protect the primary contact from arcing, so a low contact resistance will be established a millisecond later.

11.2. APPLICATIONS

- Lighting control
- Magnetic starter
- Vacuum contactor
- Mercury relay
- Mercury-wetted relay

11. 1 CONTACTOR

CHAPTER TWELVE

RAIL CONNECTOR

12.1 FEATURES:

Rail connector serves the purpose of connecting or supporting the electrical materials like contactors, circuit breakers such as miniature circuit breaker single phase etc.,.In our project we have used the rail connector to support the eight contactors which are used to connect the load. The rail connector are fitted to the hylem sheet which will be provided inside the panel.

FIG 12.1 DIN RAIL

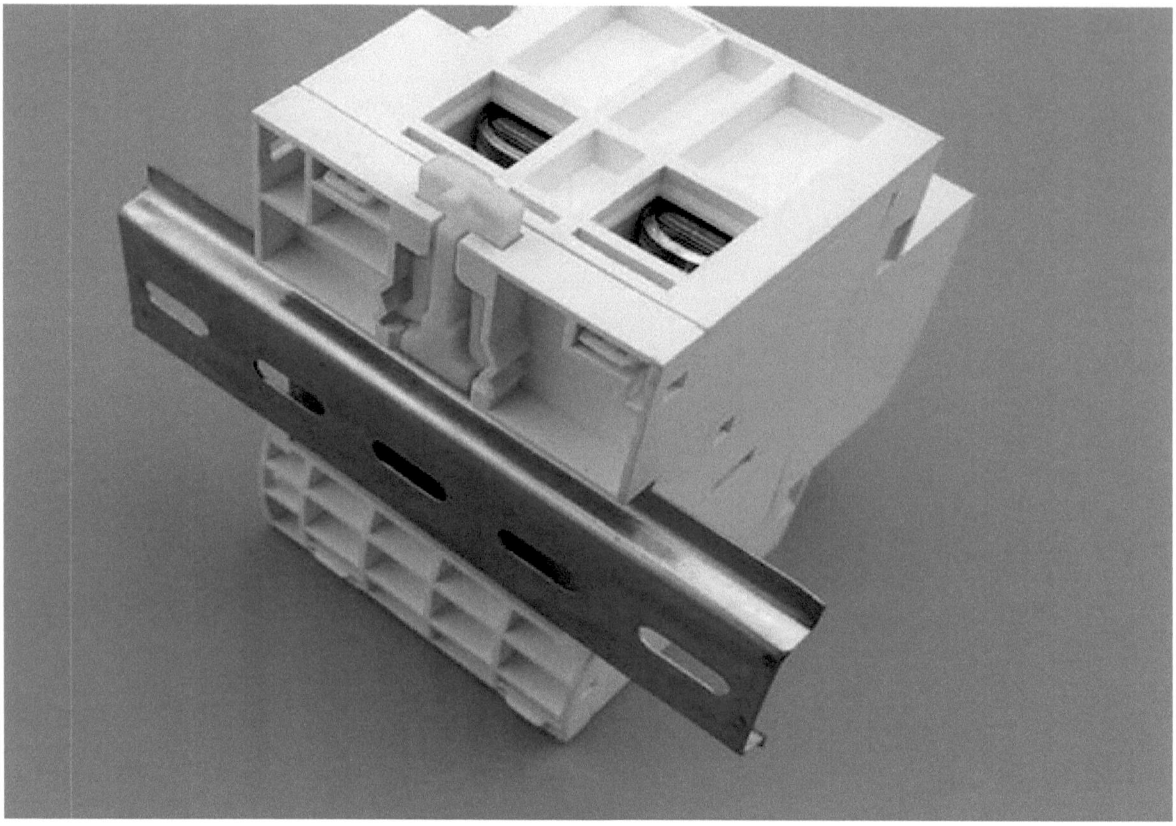

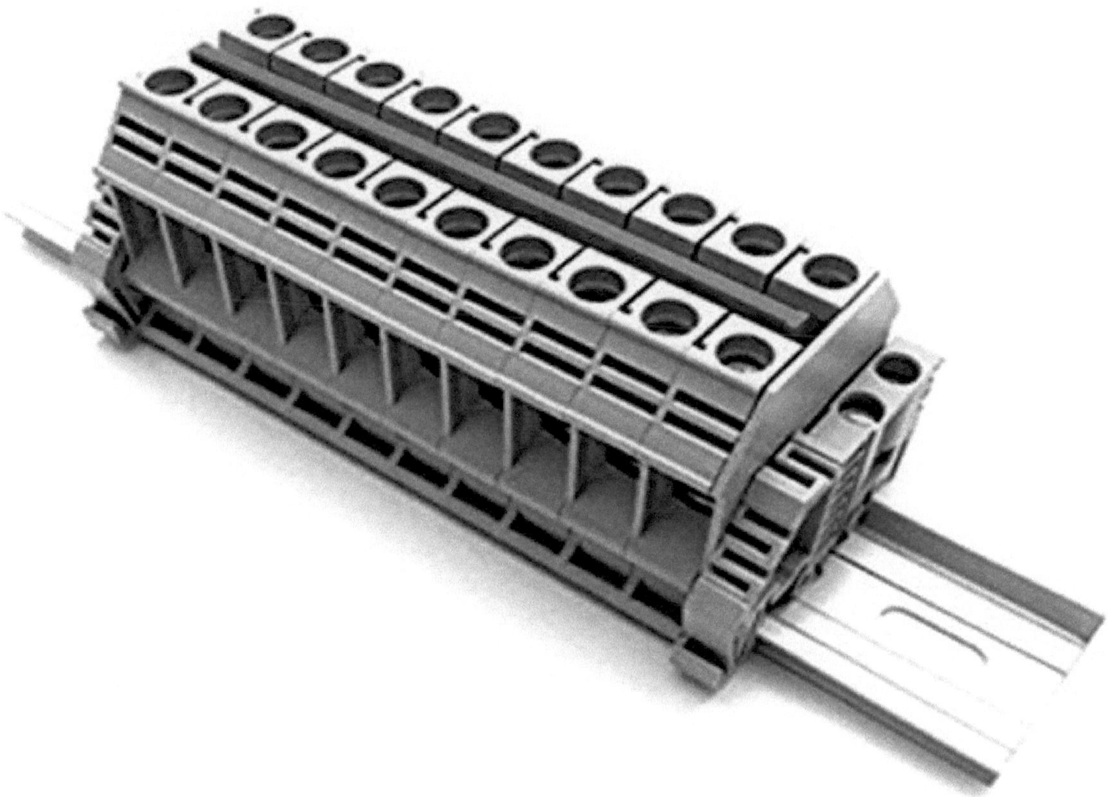

CHAPTER THIRTEEN

INDICATORS

13.1. CORE FEATURES

Indicator is a simple piece of electronic test equipment used to determine the presence or absence of an electric voltage (usually alternating current (AC) in a piece of equipment under test. A test light is generally simpler and less cost.

Commonly used colour codes for machine state conditions include:

- RED: Failure conditions such as an emergency stop or machine fault
- YELLOW: Warnings such as over-temperature or over-pressure conditions
- GREEN: Normal machine or process operation
- BLUE: External help request, where an operator might be requesting raw materials, scheduling or maintenance personnel assistanc
-

13.2. APPLICATIONS

i. Productivity monitoring
v. Warning indication
v. Lean manufacturing
v. Assembly station work cells

FIG 13.1 LOAD INDICATOR

CHAPTER FOURTEEN

PANNEL

14.1 FEATURES:

An electrical panel is also called a load centre. It is a metal electrical service box that accepts the main power to the home and distributes electrical current to the various circuits within the home.

The distribution of power to the various circuits are protected from over-current by the use of circuit breaker or fuses.

Once you open the door to the panel you can access all the circuit breakers or fuses.

In our project we have used the panel under particular dimensions where all the materials can be kept inside. As mentioned earlier inside the panel we have used eight contactors, base plate which consists of ac to dc converter to power up the RF receiver, and IOT is also fixed inside the panel. Drilling has been done to give the input mains supply and similarly other holes are made to take the wires out to connect the load.

FIG 14.1 PANEL BOX

CHAPTER FIFTEEN

HYLEM SHEET

15.1. CORE FEATURES

i. Light in weight,
v. SRBF grade has great mechanical properties, and
v. Resistant to water and chemical.

15.2. APPLICATIONS

- Gears,
- Textile shuttles,
- Bearings,
- Pickers,
- Bushes and
- Marine application

FIG 15.1 3MM HYLEM SHEET

CHAPTER SIXTEEN

REMOTE

16.1. CORE FEATURES

A handheld, wireless device used to operate audio, video and other electronic equipment using radio frequency transmission. Unlike the common infrared remotes, RF remotes do not have to be aimed at the equipment.

The greatest advantage to radio-frequency remotes is their range: They can transmit up to 100 feet from the receiver and radio signals can go through walls. These remotes use RF-to-IR converters to extend the range of an infrared remote.

When we press any key in the remote, the transmitter section generates the corresponding RF signal and this signal is received by the receiver section, hence it switches the corresponding appliance.

A four channel encoder/decoder pair is used in this system. The input signals at the transmitter section are taken from the four switches and the output signals at the receiver are indicated by the four LED's corresponding to each switch.

Here, the encoder HT12E is used to convert parallel data to serial. This data is transmitted serially to receiver point through RF.RF receiver receives the data serially and then gives to the HT12D decoder to convert it to the parallel. Four LEDs indicate the received data.

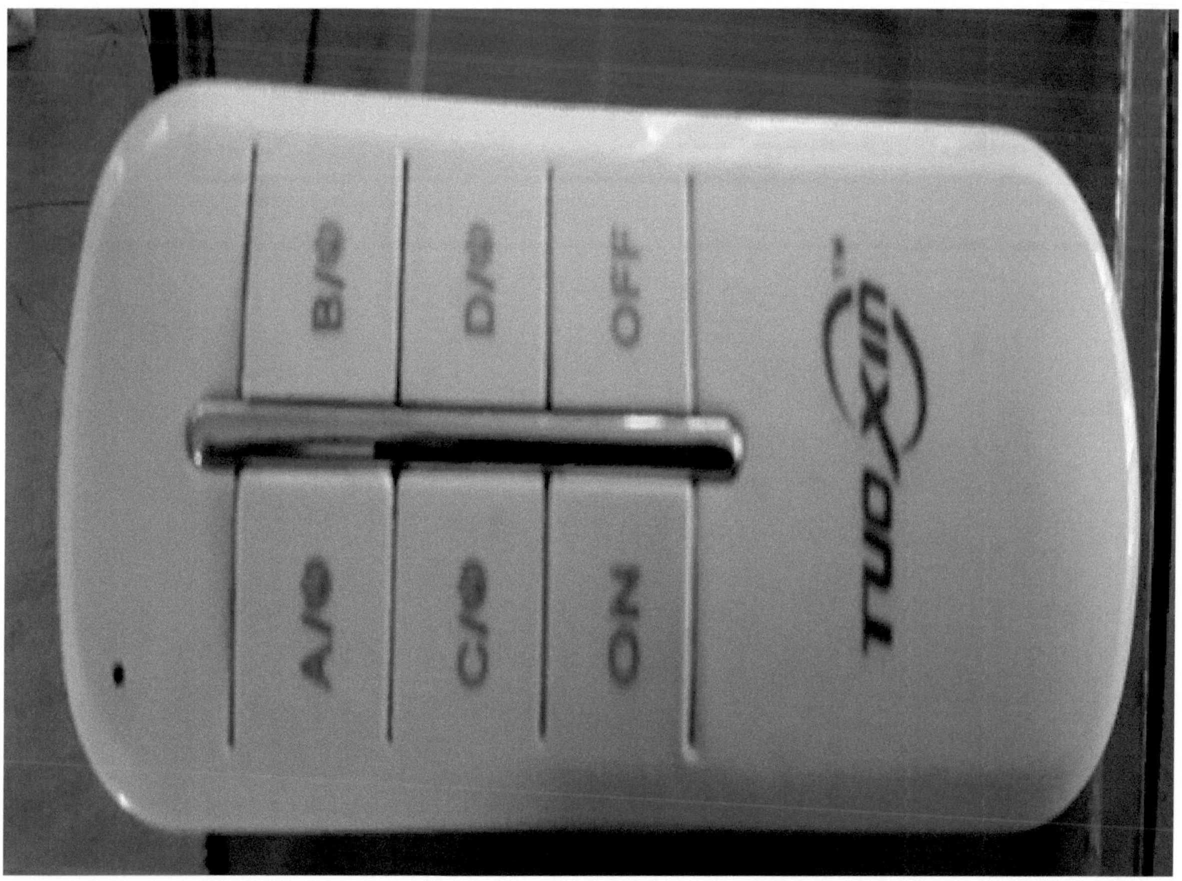

16.1 TRANSMITTER REMOTE

16.2 CIRCUIT DIAGRAM:

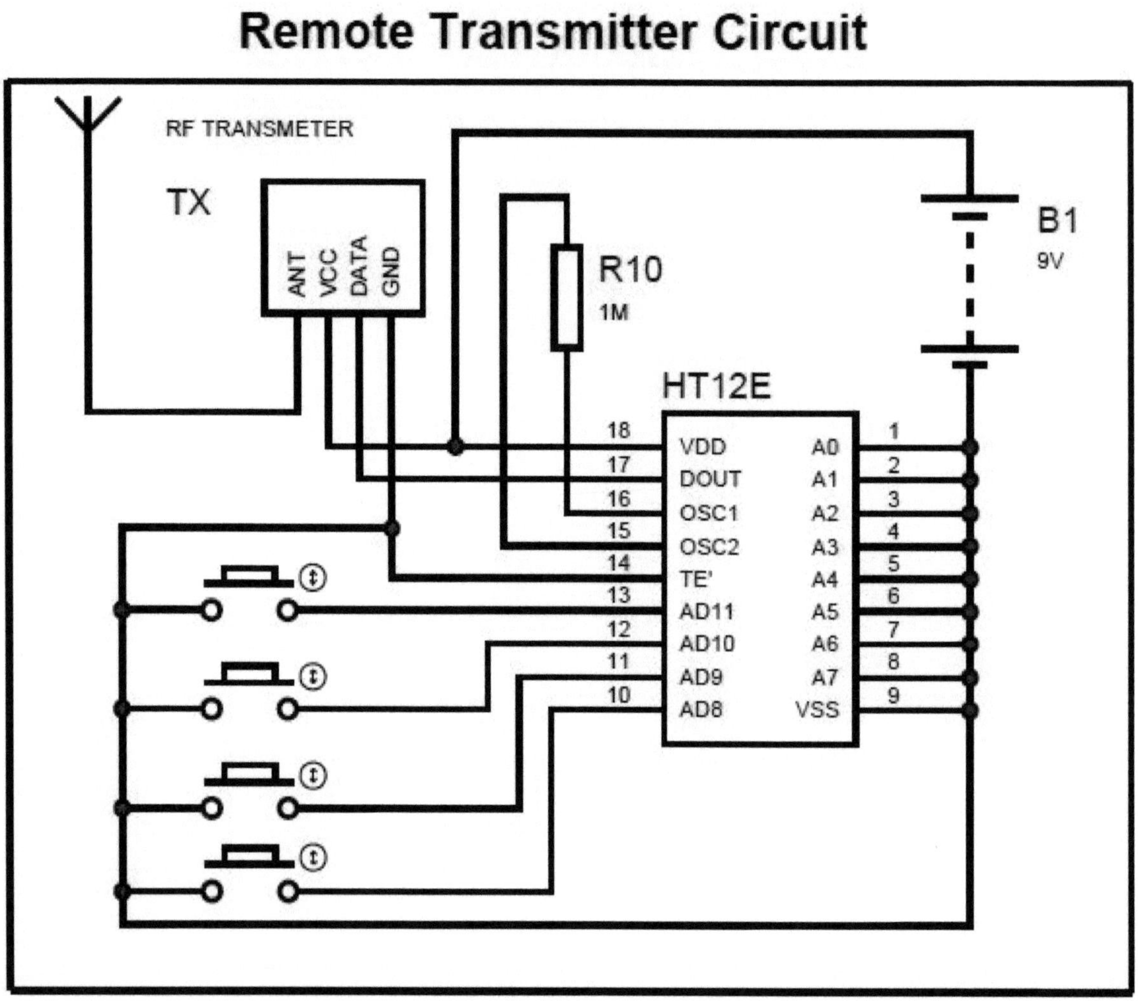

CHAPTER SEVENTEEN

CONCLUSION

The gift of technology to mankind is to make life simpler. In this work, a remote control for multiple home appliances is designed, presented and implemented. The design is durable, robust and sturdy which is built with an available compact IC's, IOT and RF module. This design combines both the technology of RF and IOT also with manual control which is new. From any place around the house any eight appliances can be controlled at will without the requirement of line of sight. The relay action which is connected to the load to be controlled is operated with radio frequency which transmits only when a switch is pressed. Multiple devices can be control using different receiver with different addressing mode using single remote. This product is used for both industrial and domestic purpose.

Printed by Libri Plureos GmbH in Hamburg,
Germany

9 798886 296877